SWEET
WILD WORLD

There is a sweet wild world which lies along the strain of the wood thrush—

May 31, 1850

HENRY DAVID THOREAU

SWEET WILD WORLD

Selections from THE JOURNALS
arranged as poetry by
WILLIAM M. WHITE

Introduction by STEVE ADAMS
Illustrations by GEORGIA DEARBORN

CHARLES RIVER BOOKS
BOSTON

Library of Congress Cataloging in Publication Data
Thoreau, Henry David, 1817-1862.
  Sweet, wild world.

  Includes index.
  1. Thoreau, Henry David, 1817-1862 – Diaries. 2. Authors,
American – 19th century – Biography. 3. Nature – Poetry.
I. White, William M. II. Title.
PS3053.A2 1982 818′.303 [B] 82-9566
ISBN 0-89182-059-0
ISBN 0-89182-060-4 (pbk.)

Published by Charles River Books, Inc.
One Thompson Square, Charlestown, MA 02129
Library of Congress Catalog Card Number
82-9566

ISBN 0 89182 059 0 (clothbound edition)
ISBN 0 89182 060 4 (paperback edition)
Printed in the United States of America

*To Audrey, Billy,
Carol, Gail,
and Katy*

ACKNOWLEDGEMENTS

I express appreciation and warmest regards to Dennis M. Campbell, Editorial Director of Charles River Books, for his personal interest in SWEET WILD WORLD. His enthusiasm, sound judgement and imagination in recent months have been central to the shaping of this book. A special thanks to my colleague, friend, Thoreau scholar and fellow Thoreau buff, Steve Adams, for his unusual and insightful introduction. Thanks to Leota Williams for her accurate typing of the manuscript. Finally, a strong note of thanks to Georgia Dearborn for her sensitive and harmonious illustrations of the Nature which Thoreau saw so clearly and loved so deeply.

CONTENTS

PREFACE

JUDGED BY THE STANDARDS of the typical American success story, Henry David Thoreau's life was a spectacular failure. Here is a man who died prior to his forty-fifth birthday, who accumulated few worldly goods, who never really had a profession, whose writings sold poorly and earned him little money or recognition. Yet Thoreau is the man to whom young people, and those who are young in spirit, have turned for pleasure, assurance and inspiration. He has the solidity of the turtle, the range of the eagle, the grace of the fox, and the musical voice of the songbird.

Most of Thoreau's poetry published during his own life tends to be rather static, old-fashioned, and either too generalized and philosophical or else overtly sentimental. There are, at best, some dozen Thoreau poems of high literary quality; and even these, hampered by their classical restraint, lack the intensity and vigor and vision of the man himself.

It is in the fourteen-volume, two-million-word *Journals*, which he kept from 1837 to 1861, that Thoreau's style relaxed into poetic cadences as natural as the flowing brooks of his native New England. His crystal-sharp and highly unusual images, his precise eye for all that was around him or within him, his love of Nature and of freedom and of wildness, his tremendous integrity – all these come forth with a clarity and force unequalled by any other nature poet in the English language. These poems do not take us back in time; they take us forward into the innermost depths of our own being.

All the poems of *Sweet Wild World* are arranged from the *Journals*, and not one word is omitted nor one mark of punctuation altered. In this book, I have taken the liberty of beginning or ending some few of the poems in the middle of a Thoreau sentence. But from first word to last, every passage is intact and every word is Thoreau's. Also, I have followed a standard nineteenth-century practice of capitalizing the opening word of each line.

For Thoreau there was no such thing as good weather or bad weather. Each day offered its own message to be absorbed and appreciated at its own tempo. This loafer was far more alive and far more productive than the busy townspeople who scurried around him. He was content to farm his own soil, and the *Journals* are the harvest of his crop. By tuning himself to the universal harmonies of Nature, he saw and felt and savored patterns and beauties in the natural environment which so many of us rush past with our heads down and to which so many of us are unfortunately blinded.

All of Nature was alive for Thoreau. He felt the pain of a chopper's axe and heard the death groan of the falling tree. Every bird, every animal, even the insects—each had its place to fill, its functional role in the totality of Nature. Each was to be enjoyed, to be studied for what it could teach, to be reverenced and held forever afterwards in the affections.

Although all of Nature was his bride, Thoreau always had an abiding interest and a very special love for birds of all kinds—from the tiny chickadee to the free-soaring eagle. Especially did he tune himself to their rills of melody. Just as no sound in nature was more basic and reassuring to him than the earthy chirping of the cricket, no music made by man or by instruments could ever approach the beauty of the wood thrush's singing. Each bird, animal and insect was special to Thoreau, and he captured them all without ever once touching them or harming them in any way. And this is as it should be.

These poems arranged from the *Journals* lead us away from the externals and accidents of life. They direct us home—direct us into our timeless selves. Thoreau understood and expressed this interior voyaging better than anyone else. As we lose ourselves in the firm beauty of the poems, we find ourselves. He shows us where to look, how to look, what to look for. He challenges us to simplify our lives and to begin to learn to see.

—William M. White

INTRODUCTION

ONE COLD, BLUSTERY DAY last January I spotted a bird that I had never seen before. Looking from an upstairs window, I saw pecking away in the snow beneath the feeder a round, fat, dull black, white-billed thing, much larger than the finches and sparrows who are our usual customers. I shuffled through the field guide but couldn't locate anything remotely resembling the bird below me. Perhaps, I thought, the winds have blown some exotic foreigner off course, or maybe I've discovered some new species.

My imagined tenure in the ornithological Hall of Fame was brief. I mistakenly decided to share the discovery with my wife, who immediately identified the stranger as a junco with feathers unusually puffed out against the wind and bitter cold. Sure enough, examining the bird through binoculars at a ground floor window revealed the white belly and slate-gray head, back and breast of the very common bird that I had looked at hundreds of times but had never before really seen. The new perspective and the slight strangeness in the bird made me study it closely for the first time. Although I felt foolish for mistaking the ordinary, I was grateful for the experience which made me see something freshly and intensely.

I feel the same way reading *Sweet Wild World*, Bill White's second volume of poetically arranged passages from Thoreau's *Journals*. As in the well received first volume, *All Nature is My Bride* (The Chatham Press, 1975), the subjects here are mostly common, quite by design. As Thoreau insisted in his journal for August 28, 1851, "I omit the unusual—the hurricanes and earthquakes—and describe the common. This has the greatest charm and is the true theme of poetry." Thoreau turns ordinary objects into poetry first by making us aware of them—by calling to our attention what frequently escapes us because it is so familiar:

The little peeping frogs make a background
Of sound in the horizon,
Which you do not hear
Unless you attend.

He makes us attend to common things and he elevates them by presenting them in new ways. He adds that element of strangeness, that new perspective or unusual way of seeing, that is one role of metaphor.

Through Thoreau's eyes, we see eagles as "kites without strings," and we watch the yellow throat of a bullfrog swell up "like a small moon at a distance." The setting sun is

A round red disk shorn of his beams, –
His head shaved like a captive led forth for execution.

Touch-me-not seed-vessels go off like pistols in Thoreau's hat. A skunk runs

With a singular teeter or undulation,
Like the walk of a Chinese lady.

Sweet Wild World is full of such startling glimpses into the commonplace, such precisely, poetically observed details. Here you will find the birds that Thoreau loved so (he preferred, he said, the "chickadee-dees" to the "D.D.'s" – the Doctors of Divinity): plovers, shrikes, chewinks, veeries, hen hawks, pine warblers, wood thrushes. In fascinating vignettes and anecdotes, an owl barks at Thoreau and a nighthawk, protecting its nest, attacks him "like an imp of darkness." He notes "how naturally anger sits on the young hawk's head" and he hears the trills of bluebirds

Reminding of so many corkscrews
Assaulting and thawing the torpid mass of winter,
Assisting the ice and snow to melt
And the streams to flow.

The book also features other inhabitants of Thoreau's world – foxes, muskrats, deer mice, snapping turtles, crickets, glow worms – and the vegetation that forms the background of his *Journals* and often steps forward to take a central role: lichens, andromeda, blue spruce, cinquefoil, houstonia, wild cherries and wild apples. People, too, are part of Thoreau's sweet wild world. He tells of an old Irishwoman who lives so close to the earth that "she will not have far to go to be buried" and he overhears his Aunt Maria complain that Henry

> stood half an hour to-day to hear the frogs croak
> And he wouldn't read the life of Chalmers.

More often than not, people bring out the prickly side of Thoreau. The portraits here include satires on "barren accomplished gentlemen," mercantile Boston, and "tender-hearted ladies" who wear "armor" stripped from the backs of animals.

Sweet Wild World is arranged, like Thoreau's masterpiece *Walden*, not by strict chronology but by seasons. One so close to nature as Thoreau was develops cycles that match nature's, and we can trace here what each of the seasons meant for Thoreau. November, for example, he called the "Eat-heart" month – a period of physical and often spiritual barrenness:

> Nothing but the echo of your steps over the frozen ground,
> No voice of birds nor frogs.

In contrast, Spring, providing here the largest number of selections, was a time of fertile profusion for both nature and Thoreau. He is especially sensitive to atmospheric conditions, and we can watch the air and sky change as Bill White takes us through Thoreau's seasons, selecting the best from what Thoreau calls his "meteorological journal of the mind."

The portraits, vignettes, and brief stories here are fascinating for the wildlife depicted, but Thoreau rarely rests content to offer what he calls "mere facts." In his journal for May 10, 1853, he says, "If I am overflowing with life, am rich in experience for which I lack expression, then nature will be my language full of poetry, – all nature will *fable*, and every natural phenomenon be a myth...I pray for such inward experience as will make nature significant." Bill White has highlighted those parts of the *Journals* in which facts flower into poetry – in which experience becomes inward, mythic, and significant. Thoreau tells, for example, of rescuing a toad from the jaws of a snake:

And I thought, as the toad jumped leisurely away
With his slime-covered hind-quarters glistening in the sun,
As if I, his deliverer, wished to interrupt his meditations, –
Without a shriek or fainting, –
I thought what a healthy indifference he manifested.
Is not this the broad earth still? he said.

Seeing a bright red tanager deep in green pines, Thoreau says,

I am transported,
These are not the woods I ordinarily walk in.

I feel the same way experiencing these poems from Thoreau's *Journals*. Although I have read the complete *Journals* and reread parts many times, I am transported by what Bill White has done to his selections. With an even surer touch than he showed in his first volume, Bill has arranged Thoreau's lines to bring out their poetic qualities – the assonance and alliteration, the subtle rhythms and cadences, sometimes even the rhymes – that are easy to miss when these passages of heightened language are read (often too quickly) amid the flatter, prosaic journal entries. According to Thoreau, "How much, what infinite, leisure it requires . . . to appreciate a single phenomenon!" With his arrangements here, Bill White has provided the leisure needed to appreciate phenomena from Thoreau's perspective. The breaks in the lines give us pause for reflection; the margins provide space for Thoreau's words to resonate. Experiencing these glimpses into Thoreau's sweet wild world, we do not wonder that, even on his deathbed, he refused to speculate on an afterlife. We *know* why he insisted, "One world at a time."

–STEVE ADAMS
BLACKSBURG, VA

SWEET
WILD WORLD

SUMMER

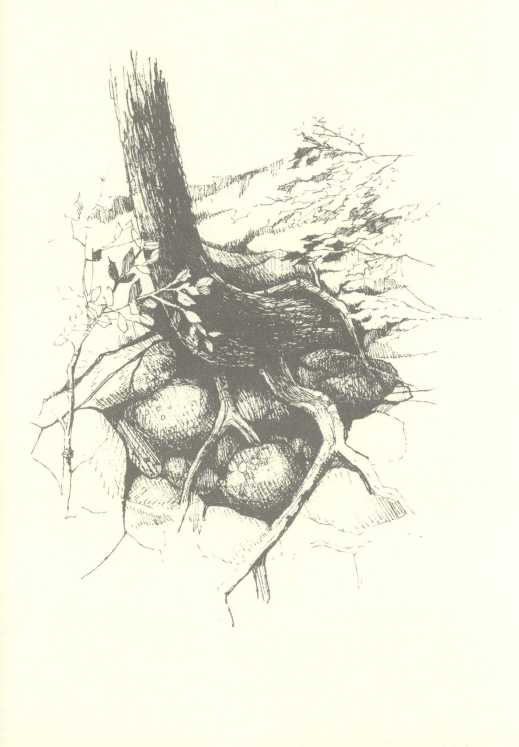

JUNE

JUNE

The sound of the crickets at dawn
After these first sultry nights
Seems like the dreaming of the earth
Still continued into the daylight.

I love that early twilight hour
When the crickets still creak right on
With such dewy faith and promise,
As if it were still night, —
Expressing the innocence of morning, —
When the creak of the cricket is fresh and bedewed.

When the creak of the cricket
Has that ambrosial sound,
No crime can be committed.
It buries Greece and Rome past resurrection.
The earth-song of the cricket!
Before Christianity was, it is.

There is no motion nor sound in the woods
(Hubbard's Grove) along which I am walking.
The trees stand like great screens against the sky.

The distant village sounds are the barking of dogs,
That animal with which man has allied himself,
And the rattling of wagons,
For the farmers have gone into town a-shopping
This Saturday night.
The dog is the tamed wolf,
As the villager is the tamed savage.

But near, the crickets are heard in the grass,
Chirping from everlasting to everlasting,
A mosquito sings near my ear,
And the humming of a dor-bug
Drowns all the noise of the village,
So roomy is the universe.

JUNE

I long for wildness,
A nature which I cannot put my foot through,
Woods where the wood thrush forever sings,
Where the hours are early morning ones,
And there is dew on the grass,
And the day is forever unproved,
Where I might have a fertile unknown for a soil about me.

I am off the handle, as the phrase is, —
I begin to be transcendental and show where my heart is.
I am like those guinea-fowl
Which Charles Darwin saw at the Cape de Verd Islands.

He says,
"They avoided us like partridges
On a rainy day in September,
Running with their heads cocked up;
And if pursued,
They readily took to the wing."

Keep your distance,
Do not infringe on the interval between us,
And I will pick up lime
And lay real terrestrial eggs for you,
And let you know by cackling
When I have done it.

JUNE

At the base of some hellebore,
In a tuft a little from under the east edge of an apple tree,
Below violet wood-sorrel,
A nest well made outside of leaves,
Then grass, lined with fine grass,
Very deep and narrow, with thick sides,
With four small somewhat cream-colored eggs
With small brown and some black spots
Chiefly toward larger end.
The bird, which flew off quickly,
Made me think of a wren
And of a Maryland yellow-throat,
Though I saw no yellow.

The small green bittern
Would now and then sail away on sluggish wings
From some recess of the shore.

With its patient study by rocks and sandy capes,
Has it wrested the whole of her secret from Nature yet?

It has looked out from its dull eye for so long,
Standing on one leg,
On moon and stars sparkling through silence and dark,
And now what a rich experience is its!

What says it of stagnant pools,
And reeds,
And damp night fogs?

It would be worth while to look in the eye
Which has been open and seeing at such hours
And in such solitudes.
When I behold that dull yellowish green,
I wonder if my own soul is not a bright, invisible green,
I would fain lay my eye side by side with its
And learn of it.

The piping plover,
As it runs half invisible on the sand before you,
Utters a shrill peep on an elevated key
(Different birds on different keys),
As if to indicate its locality from time to time to its kind,
Or it utters a succession of short notes
As it flies low over the sand or water.
Ever and anon stands still tremblingly,
Or teeteringly,
Wagtail-like,
Turning this way and that.

JUNE

In the very open park in the rear of the Rocks on the hilltop,
Where lambkill and huckleberries and grass alternate,
Came to one of those handsome, round,
Mirror-like pools a rod or two in diameter
And surrounded with a border of fine weeds,
Such as you frequently meet with
On the top of springy hills.

Though warm and muddy at bottom,
They are very beautiful and glassy
And look as if they were cool springs;
So high, exposed to the light,
Yet so wild and fertile,
As if the fertility of the lowland was transferred
To the summit of the hills.

These are the kind of mirrors
At which the huntresses in the golden age
Arranged their toilets,
Which the deer frequented
And contemplated their branching horns in.

The rose-breasted grosbeak is common now
In the Flint's Pond woods.
It is not at all shy,
And our richest singer, perhaps,
After the wood thrush.

The rhythm is very like that of the tanager,
But the strain is perfectly clear and sweet.
One sits on the bare dead twig of a chestnut,
High over the road, at Gourgas Wood, and over my head,
And sings clear and loud at regular intervals, –
The strain about ten or fifteen seconds long,
Rising and swelling to the end,
With various modulations.

Another, singing in emulation, regularly answers it,
Alternating with it, from a distance,
At least a quarter of a mile off.
It sings thus long at a time,
And I leave it singing there.

JUNE

Would it not be a luxury to stand up to one's chin
In some retired swamp for a whole summer's day,
Scenting the sweet-fern and bilberry blows,
And lulled by the minstrelsy of gnats and mosquitoes?
A day passed in the society of those Greek sages,
Such as described in the "Banquet" of Xenophon,
Would not be comparable
With the dry wit of decayed cranberry vines,
And the fresh Attic salt of the moss beds.
Say twelve hours of genial and familiar converse
With the leopard frog.

The sun to rise behind alder and dogwood,
And climb bouyantly to his meredian of three hands' breadth,
And finally sink to rest behind some bold western hummock.
To hear the evening chant of the mosquito
From a thousand green chapels,
And the bittern begin to boom from his concealed fort
Like a sunset gun!

The bullfrogs lie on the very surface of the pads,
Showing their great yellow throats,
Color of the yellow breeches of the old school,
And protuberant eyes.

His whole back out,
Revealing a vast expanse of belly.
His eyes like ranunculus or yellow lily buds,
Winking from time to time
And showing his large dark-bordered tympanum.
Imperturbable-looking.

His yellow throat swells up
Like a small moon at a distance.

Saw its two eggs on the bare ground,
On a slight shelf of the hill,
On the dead pine-needles and sand,
Without any cavity or nest whatever,
Very obvious when once you had detected them,
But not easily detected from their color,
A coarse gray formed of white
Spotted with a bluish or slaty brown or umber, —
A stone — granite — color, like the places it selects.

I advanced and put my hand on them,
And while I stooped,
Seeing a shadow on the ground,
Looked up and saw the bird,
Which had fluttered down the hill so blind and helpless,
Circling low and swiftly past over my head,
Showing the white spot on each wing
In true nighthawk fashion.

When I had gone a dozen rods,
It appeared again higher in the air,
With its peculiar flitting, limping kind of flight,
All the while noiseless,
And suddenly descending,
It dashed at me within ten feet of my head,
Like an imp of darkness.

A nighthawk is circling, imp-like,
With undulating, irregular flight
Over the sprout-land on the Cliff Hill,
With an occasional squeak
And showing the spots on his wings.

He does not circle away from this place,
And I associate him with two gray eggs
Somewhere on the ground beneath
And a mate there sitting.

The old bird was uttering that hoarse worried note
From time to time,
Somewhat like a partridge's,
Flying past from side to side
And alighting amid the trees or bushes.

When I had descended,
I detected one young one two thirds grown
Perched on a branch of the next tree,
About fifteen feet from the ground,
Which was all the while staring at me
With its great yellow eyes.

It was gray with gray horns and a dark beak.
As I walked past near it, it turned its head steadily,
Always facing me, without moving its body,
Till it looked directly the opposite way over its back,
But never offered to fly.

Just then I thought surely that I heard a puppy
Faintly barking at me four or five rods distant
Amid the bushes, having tracked me into the swamp, —
What what, what what what.
It was exactly such a noise
As the barking of a very small dog or perhaps a fox.
But it was the old owl,
For I presently saw her making it.

The sun not yet set.
The bobolink sings descending to the meadow
As I go along the railroad to the pond.
The seringo-bird and the common song sparrow, –
And the swallows twitter.
The plaintive strain of the lark,
Coming up from the meadow,
Is perfectly adapted to the hour.

When I get nearer the wood,
The veery is heard,
And the oven-bird, or whet-saw, sounds hollowly
From within the recesses of the wood.

The clouds in the west are edged with fiery red.
A few robins faintly sing.
The huckleberry-bird in more open fields in the woods.
The thrasher?

The sun is down.
The nighthawks are squeaking
In the somewhat dusky air
And occasionally making the ripping sound;
The chewinks sound;
The bullfrogs begin.

JULY

Every bush and vine teems with palatable fruit.
Man for once stands in such relation to Nature
As the animals that pluck and eat as they go.
The fields and hills are a table constantly spread.

Wines of all kinds and qualities, of noblest vintage,
Are bottled up in the skins of countless berries,
For the taste of men and animals.

To men they seem offered not so much for food
As for sociality, that they may picnic with Nature, –
Diet drinks, cordials, wines.
We pluck and eat in remembrance of Her.
It is a sacrament, a communion.

A boy is looking after his cows,
Calling "ker ker ker ker," impatient to go home.
The sun is passing under the portcullis of the west.

The nighthawk squeaks,
And the chewink jingles his strain,
And the wood thrush;
But I think
There is no loud and general serenade from the birds.
I hear no veery.
How much more swiftly the sun seems to perform
The morning and evening portions of his journey,
When he is nearest his starting-place or goal!

He is now almost ready to dip, –
A round red disk shorn of his beams, –
His head shaved like a captive led forth for execution.

JULY

I hear the sound of Heywood's Brook
Falling into Fair Haven Pond,
Inexpressibly refreshing to my senses.
It seems to flow through my very bones.

I hear it with insatiable thirst.
It allays some sandy heat in me.
It affects my circulations;
Methinks my arteries have sympathy with it.

What is it I hear but the pure waterfalls within me,
In the circulation of my blood,
The streams that fall into my heart?
What mists do I ever see
But such as hang over and rise from my blood?

The sound of this gurgling water,
Running thus by night as by day,
Falls on all my dashes,
Fills all my buckets,
Overflows my float-boards,
Turns all the machinery of my nature,
Makes me a flume, a sluice-way,
To the springs of nature.

Thus I am washed;
Thus I drink and quench my thirst.

JULY

We sit on the edge of the hill at the Jenkins house,
Looking northward over a retired dell in the woods,
An unfrequented johnswort and blackberry field,
Surrounded by a deep forest —
With several tall white pines against the horizon,
A study of which you would never tire.

The swallows twitter overhead,
The locust, we know not where, is z-ing,
And the huckleberry-bird is heard on the birches.

The ground under the apple tree, where we lie,
Is strewn with small sun-baked apples,
But we are not yet reminded of apples.

When life looks sandy and barren,
Is reduced to its lowest terms,
We have no appetite, and it has no flavor,
Then let me visit such a swamp as this,
Deep and impenetrable,
Where the earth quakes for a rod around you
At every step,
With its open water
Where the swallows skim and twitter,
Its meadow and cotton-grass,
Its dense patches of dwarf andromeda,
Now brownish-green,
With clumps of blueberry bushes,
Its spruces and its verdurous border of woods
Imbowering it on every side.

At last nearly stumbled on to a young hawk.
There was one big as my fist,
Resting on the bare, flat nest in the sun,
With a great head, staring eyes,
And open gaping or panting mouth,
Yet mere down, grayish-white down, as yet;
But I detected another
Which had crawled a foot one side amid the bushes
For shade or safety, more than half as large again,
With small feathers and a yet more angry, hawk-like look.
How naturally anger sits on the young hawk's head.

Pratt says he one day walked out with Wesson,
With their rifles, as far as Hunt's Bridge.
Looking downstream,
He saw a swallow sitting on a bush very far off,
At which he took aim and fired with ball.

He was surprised to see that he had touched the swallow,
For it flew directly across the river
Toward Simon Brown's barn,
Always descending toward the earth or water,
Not being able to maintain itself;

But what surprised him most was to see a second swallow
Come flying behind
And repeatedly strike the other with all his force beneath,
So as to toss him up as often as he approached the ground
And enable him to continue his flight,
And thus he continued to do till they were out of sight.

Pratt said he resolved
That he would never fire at a swallow again.

And now the evening redness deepens
Till all the west or northwest horizon is red;
As if the sky were rubbed there
With some rich Indian pigment,
A permanent dye;
As if the Artist of the world
Had mixed his red paints
On the edge of the inverted saucer of the sky.

An exhilarating, cheering redness, most wholesome.
There should be a red race of men.
I would look into the west at this hour
Till my face permanently reflects that red.
It is like the stain of some berries
Crushed along the edge of the sky.

To-day I met with the first orange flower of autumn.
What means this doubly torrid, this Bengal, tint?
Yellow took sun enough,
But this is the fruit of a dog-day sun.
The year has but just produced it.

Here is the Canada thistle in bloom,
Visited by butterflies and bees.
The butterflies have swarmed within these few days,
Especially about the milkweeds.
The swamp-pink still fills the air with its perfume
In swamps and by the causeways, though it is far gone.
The wild rose still scatters its petals
Over the leaves of neighboring plants.

The wild morning-glory or bindweed,
With its delicate red and white blossoms.
I remember it ever as a goblet full of purest morning air
And sparkling with dew,
Showing the dew-point,
Winding round itself for want of other support.
It grows by the Hubbard Bridge causeway,
Near the angelica.

The cherry-birds are making their *seringo* sound
As they flit past.
They soon find out the locality of the cherry trees.
And beyond the bridge there is a goldenrod
Partially blossomed.
Yesterday it was spring,
And to-morrow it will be autumn.

AUGUST

The vials of summer never made a man sick,
But those which he stored in his cellar.
Drink the wines,
Not of your bottling,
But Nature's bottling;
Not kept in goat-skins or pig-skins,
But the skins of a myriad fair berries.

The whole surface of the earth is now streaked
With wreaths of fog over meadow and forest,
Alternating with the green.

The sun, now working round the Cliffs,
Fires his rays into the battalions of fog
Which are collected over Fair Haven Pond
And have taken refuge on the west side of the Hill;
Routs and disperses them.

A dewy, cobwebbed morning.
You observe the geometry of cobwebs,
Though most are of that gossamer character,
Close woven,
As if a fairy had dropt her veil on the grass in the night.

What is a New England landscape this sunny August day?
A weather-painted house and barn,
With an orchard by its side,
In midst of a sandy field surrounded by green woods,
With a small blue lake on one side.
A sympathy between the color of the weather-painted house
And that of the lake and sky.

I speak not of a country road between its fences,
For this house lies off one,
Nor do I commonly approach them from this side.
The weather-painted house.
This is the New England color,
Homely but fit as that of a toadstool.

What matter though this one
Has not been inhabited for thirty years?
Methinks I hear the crow of a cock
Come up from its barn-yard.

AUGUST

As I go home by Hayden's
I smell the burning meadow.
I love the scent.
It is my pipe.
I smoke the earth.

I go to bed and dream of cranberry-pickers
Far in the cold north.
With windows partly closed,
With continent concentrated thoughts,
I dream.

I get my new experiences still,
Not at the opera listening to the Swedish Nightingale,
But at Beck Stow's Swamp
Listening to the native wood thrush.

I hear the foxes trotting about me over the dead leaves,
And now gently over the grass,
As if not to disturb the dew which is falling.

Why should we not
Cultivate neighborly relations with the foxes?

As if to improve upon our seeming advances,
Comes one to greet us nosewise under our tent-curtain.
Nor do we rudely repulse him.
Is man powder
And the fox flint and steel?

Has not the time come
When men and foxes shall lie down together?

Has not the tortoise also learned the true value of time?
You go to India and back,
And the turtle eggs in your field are still unhatched.
French empires rise or fall,
But the turtle is developed only so fast.
What's a summer?
Time for a turtle's eggs to hatch.

So is the turtle developed,
Fitted to endure,
For he outlives twenty French dynasties.
One turtle knows several Napoleons.

AUGUST

I saw a snake by the roadside
And touched him with my foot to see if he were alive.
He had a toad in his jaws,
Which he was preparing to swallow
With his jaws distended to three times his width,
But he relinquished his prey in haste and fled;
And I thought, as the toad jumped leisurely away
With his slime-covered hind-quarters glistening in the sun,
As if I, his deliverer, wished to interrupt his meditations, –
Without a shriek or fainting, –
I thought what a healthy indifference he manifested.
Is not this the broad earth still? he said.

I conclude that the goldfinch
Is a very fine and powerful singer,
And the most successful
And remarkable mocking-bird that we have.

In the spring I heard it imitate the thrasher exactly,
Before that bird had arrived,
And now it imitates the purple finch as perfectly,
After the latter bird has ceased to sing!

It is a surprising vocalist.
It did not cease singing
Till I disturbed it by my nearer approach,
And then it went off with its usual *mew*,
Succeeded by its watery twitter in *ricochet* flight.

At Baker Farm a large bird rose up near us,
Which at first I took for a hen-hawk,
But it appeared larger.
It screamed the same,
And finally soared higher and higher
Till it was almost lost amid the clouds,
Or could scarcely be distinguished except when it was seen
Against some white and glowing cumulus.

I think it was at least half a mile high, or three quarters,
And yet I distinctly heard it scream up there
Each time it came round,
And with my glass saw its head
Steadily bent toward the ground,
Looking for its prey.
Its head, seen in a proper light, was distinctly whitish,
And I suspect it may have been a white-headed eagle.

It did not once flap its wings up there,
As it circled and sailed,
Though I watched it for nearly a mile.
How fit that these soaring birds should be haughty and fierce,
Not like doves to our race!

The leaves of the dogsbane are turning yellow.
There are as few or fewer birds heard
Than flowers seen.
The red-eye still occasionally.
Agrimony still.

"The dry, pearly, and almost incorruptible heads
Of the Life Everlasting."
Ah! this is a truly elysian flower now,
Beyond change and decay,
Not lusty but immortal, —
Pure ascetics, suggesting a widowed virginity.

AUGUST

I hear, low and steady, under all other sounds,
The creak of the mole cricket by the riverside.
It has a peculiarly late sound,
Suggestive of the progress of the year.
It is the voice which comes up steadily at this season
From that narrow sandy strip
Between the meadow and the water's edge.

You might think it issued from that small frog,
The only living thing you see,
Which sits so motionless on the sand.
But the singer is wholly out of sight
In his gallery under the surface.
Creak creak, creak creak, creak creak, creak creak.

It is a sound associated with the declining year
And recalls the moods of that season.
It is so unobtrusive yet universal a sound,
So underlying the other sounds which fill the air, —
The song of birds, rustling of leaves,
Dry hopping sound of grasshoppers, etc., —
That now, in my chamber,
I can hardly be sure whether I hear it still,
Or remember it,
It so rings in my ears.

AUTUMN

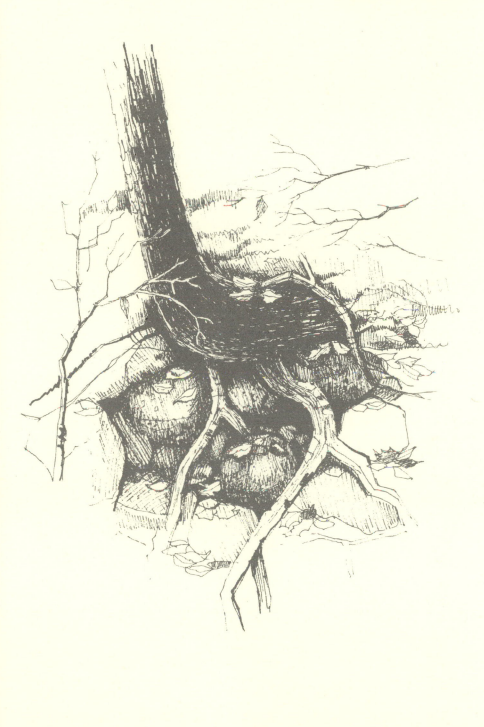

SEPTEMBER

SEPTEMBER

In this month of September,
When men are turned travellers,
Hastening to the seaside, or the mountains, or the lakes, –
In this month of travelling, –
This modest maple, having ripened its seeds,
Still without budging an inch,
Travels on its reputation,
Runs up its scarlet flag on that hillside,
To show that it has finished its summer work.

It is a luxury to muse by a wall-side
In the sunshine of a September afternoon, –
To cuddle down under a gray stone,
And hearken to the siren song of the cricket.
Day and night seem henceforth but accidents,
And the time is always a still eventide,
And as the close of a happy day.

Parched fields
And mulleins gilded with the slanting rays
Are my diet.

Moonlight on Fair Haven Pond seen from the Cliffs.
A sheeny lake in the midst of a boundless forest,
The windy surf sounding freshly and wildly
In the single pine behind you;
The silence of hushed wolves in the wilderness,
And, as you fancy,
Moose looking off from the shore of the lake.

The stars of poetry and history and unexplored nature
Looking down on the scene.
This is my world now,
With a dull whitish mark curving northward
Through the forest
Marking the outlet to the lake.

Fair Haven by moonlight lies there
Like a lake in the Maine wilderness
In the midst of a primitive forest untrodden by man.
This light and this hour
Take the civilization all out of the landscape.

Even in villages dogs bay at the moon;
In forests like this
We listen to hear wolves howl to Cynthia.

A stray white cat sits on the shore looking over the water.
This is her hour.
A nighthawk dashes past, low over the water.
This is what we had.

It was in harmony with this fair evening
That we were not walking or riding
With dust and noise through it,
But moved by a paddle without a jar
Over the liquid and almost invisible surface,
Floating directly toward those islands of the blessed
Which we call clouds in the sunset sky.

I thought of the Indian,
Who so many similar evenings had paddled up this stream,
With what advantage he beheld the twilight sky.
So we advanced without dust or sound,
By gentle influences.

Now I see a large one – perchance an eagle,
I say to myself! – down in the valley,
Circling and circling, higher and wider.
This way he comes.

How beautiful does he repose on the air,
In the moment when he is directly over you,
And you see the form and texture of his wings!

How light he must make himself,
How much earthy heaviness expel,
Before he can thus soar and sail!
He carries no useless clogs there with him.

They are out by families;
While one is circling this way,
Another circles that.
Kites without strings.
Where is the boy that flies them?

The earth nurses these eggs.
They are planted in the earth,
And the earth takes care of them;
She is genial to them
And does not kill them.

It suggests a certain vitality
And intelligence in the earth,
Which I had not realized.
This mother is not merely inanimate and inorganic.

Though the immediate mother turtle
Abandons her offspring,
The earth and sun are kind to them.
The old turtle on which the earth rests takes care of them
While the other waddles off.
Earth was not made poisonous and deadly to them.

The earth has some virtue in it;
When seeds are put into it, they germinate;
When turtles' eggs, they hatch in due time.

Green lice are still on the birches.

At Saw Mill Brook many finely cut and flat ferns are faded
Whitish and very handsome, as if pressed, – very delicate.

White oak acorns edible.
Everywhere the squirrels are trying the nuts
In good season.

The touch-me-not seed-vessels go off like pistols, –
Shoot their seeds off like bullets.
They explode in my hat.

I had always instinctively regarded the horse
As a free people somewhere, living wild.
Whatever has not come under the sway of man is wild.
In this sense original and independent men are wild, —
Not tamed and broken by society.

Now for my part
I have such a respect for the horse's nature
As would tempt me to let him alone;
Not to interfere with him, —
His walks, his diet, his loves.
But by mankind he is treated simply as if he were an engine
Which must have rest and is sensible of pain.

Suppose that every squirrel were made to turn a coffee-mill!
Suppose that the gazelles were made to draw milk-carts!

OCTOBER

Fallen leaves.
How densely they cover and conceal the water
For several feet in width, under and amid the alders
And button-bushes and maples along the shore of the river, –
Still light, tight, and dry boats,
Dense cities of boats,
Their fibres not relaxed by the waters,
Undulating and rustling with every wave,
Of such various pure and delicate, though fading, tints, –
Of hues that might make the fame of teas, –
Dried on great Nature's coppers.

And then see this great fleet of scattered leaf boats,
Still tight and dry,
Each one curled up on every side by the sun's skill,
Like boats of hide,
Scarcely moving in the sluggish current, –
Like the great fleets with which you mingle
On entering some great mart,
Some New York which we are all approaching together.

Most leaves are already somewhat faded and withered.
Their tints are not so bright.
The chestnut leaves already rustle with a great noise
As you walk through the woods,
As they lie light, firm, and crisp.

Now the chestnuts are rattling out.
The burs are gaping and showing the plump nuts.
They fill the ruts in the road, and are abundant
Amid the fallen leaves in the midst of the wood.

The jays scream,
And the red squirrels scold,
While you are clubbing and shaking the trees.
Now it is true autumn;
All things are crisp and ripe.

Thus they stand at the mouths of their burrows,
In the warm pasture, near the close of the year,
Shuffling their wing-cases over each other (the males only),
And producing this sharp but pleasant creaking sound, –
Helping to fetch the year about.
Thus the sounds of human industry and activity –
The roar of cannon, blasting of rocks,
Whistling of locomotives, rattling of carts,
Tinkering of artisans, and voices of men –
May sound to some distant ear like an earth-song
And the creaking of crickets.

Let a full-grown but young cock stand near you.
How full of life he is,
From the tip of his bill
Through his trembling wattles and comb and his bright eye
To the extremity of his clean toes!

How alert and restless,
Listening to every sound and watching every motion!
How various his notes,
From the finest and shrillest alarum as a hawk sails over,
Surpassing the most accomplished violinist
On the short strings,
To a hoarse and terrene voice or cluck!

He has a word for every occasion;
For the dog that rushes past,
And partlet cackling in the barn.
And then how, elevating himself and flapping his wings,
He gathers impetus and air
And launches forth that world-renowned ear-piercing strain!
Not a vulgar note of defiance,
But the mere effervescence of life,
Like the bursting of a bubble in a wine-cup.

The moon is too far west to be seen
Reflected in the river at Tupelo Cliff,
But the stars are reflected.

The river is a dark mirror
With bright points feebly fluctuating.
I smell the bruised horsemint,
Which I cannot see,
While I sit on the brown rocks by the shore.

I see the glow-worm under the damp cliff.
No whip-poor-wills are heard to-night,
And scarcely a note of any other bird.

At 8 o'clock the fogs have begun,
Which,
With the low half-moon shining on them,
Look like cobwebs or thin white veils
Spread over the earth.
They are the dreams or visions of the meadow.

OCTOBER

I have met with some barren accomplished gentlemen
Who seem to have been to school all their lives
And never had a vacation to live in.

Oh, if they could only have been stolen by the Gypsies!
And carried far beyond the reach of their guardians!
They had better have died in infancy
And been buried under the leaves,
Their lips besmeared with blackberries,
And Cock Robin for their sexton.

Why do you flee so soon, sir,
To the theatres, lecture-rooms, and museums of the city?
If you will stay here awhile I will promise you strange sights.

You shall walk on water;
All these brooks and rivers
And ponds shall be your highway.
You shall see the whole earth covered a foot or more deep
With purest white crystals,
In which you slump or over which you glide,
And all the trees and stubble glittering in icy armor.

The seeds of the bidens, —
Without florets, —
Or beggar-ticks,
With four-barbed awns like hay-hooks,
Now adhere to your clothes,
So that you are all bristling with them.
Certainly they adhere to nothing so readily
As to woolen cloth,
As if in the creation of them
The invention of woolen clothing by man had been foreseen.

How tenacious of its purpose to spread and plant its race!
By all methods nature secures this end,
Whether by the balloon,
Or parachute,
Or hook,
Or barbed spear like this,
Or mere lightness which the winds can waft.

I frequently pluck wild apples
Of so rich and spicy a flavor
That I wonder all orchardists do not get a scion from them,
But when I have brought home my pockets full,
And taste them in the house,
They are unexpectedly harsh, crude things.

They must be eaten in the fields,
When your system is all aglow with exercise,
The frosty weather nips your fingers (in November),
The wind rattles the bare boughs and rustles the leaves,
And the jay is heard screaming around.

OCTOBER

The weeds are dressed in their frost jackets,
Naked down to their close-fitting downy or flannel shirts.
Like athletes they challenge the winter,
These bare twigs.
This cold refines and condenses us.
Our spirits are strong,
Like that pint of cider in the middle of a frozen barrel.

This annual decay and death,
This dying by inches,
Before the whole tree at last lies down
And turns to soil.

As trees shed their leaves,
So deer their horns,
And men their hair or nails,
The year's great crop.

I am more interested in it than in the English grass alone
Or in the corn.
It prepares the virgin mould for future cornfields
On which the earth fattens.

They teach us how to die.
How many flutterings
Before they rest quietly in their graves!
A myriad wrappers for germinating seeds.

By what subtle chemistry they will mount up again,
Climbing by the sap in the trees.

NOVEMBER

Much cold, slate-colored cloud,
Bare twigs seen gleaming
Toward the light like gossamer,
Pure green of pines whose old leaves have fallen,
Reddish or yellowish brown oak leaves
Rustling on the hillsides,
Very pale brown, bleaching,
Almost hoary fine grass or hay in the fields,
Akin to the frost which has killed it,
And flakes of clear yellow sunlight
Falling on it here and there, –
Such is November.

Now is the time for wild apples.
I pluck them as a wild fruit
Native to this quarter of the earth,
Fruit of old trees that have been dying
Ever since I was a boy
And are not yet dead.

From the appearance of the tree
You would expect nothing but lichens to drop from it,
But underneath your faith is rewarded
By finding the ground strewn with spirited fruit.

Frequented only by the woodpecker,
Deserted now by the farmer,
Who has not faith enough to look under the boughs.
Food for walkers.

Sometimes apples red inside,
Perfused with a beautiful blush,
Faery food,
Too beautiful to eat, –
Apple of the evening sky,
Of the Hesperides.

I found Fair Haven skimmed entirely over,
Though the stones which I threw down on it
From the high bank on the east broke through.
Yet the river was open.

The landscape looked singularly clean and pure and dry,
The air, like a pure glass, being laid over the picture,
The trees so tidy, stripped of their leaves;
The meadows and pastures, clothed with clean dry grass,
Looked as if they had been swept;
Ice on the water and winter in the air,
But yet not a particle of snow on the ground.

The woods,
Divested in great part of their leaves,
Are being ventilated.

It is the season of perfect works,
Of hard, tough, ripe twigs,
Not of tender buds and leaves.
The leaves have made their wood,
And a myriad new withes stand up all around
Pointing to the sky,
Able to survive the cold.
It is only the perennial that you see,
The iron age of the year.

To see a remote landscape between two near rocks!
I want no other gilding to my picture-frame.

There they lie,
As perchance they tumbled and split from off an iceberg.
What better frame could you have?
The globe itself, here named pasture,
For ground and foreground,
Two great boulders for the sides of the frame,
And the sky itself for the top!
And for artists and subject, God and Nature!
Such pictures cost nothing but eyes,
And it will not bankrupt one to own them.

NOVEMBER

One must needs climb a hill to know what a world he inhabits.
In the midst of this Indian summer
I am perched on the topmost rock of Nawshawtuct,
A velvet wind blowing from the southwest.

I seem to feel the atoms as they strike my cheek.

Hills, mountains, steeples
Stand out in bold relief in the horizon,
While I am resting
On the rounded boss of an enormous shield,
The river like a vein of silver encircling its edge,
And thence the shield gradually rises to its rim,
The horizon.

Not a cloud is to be seen,
But villages, villas, forests, mountains,
One above another,
Till they are swallowed up in the heavens.

The atmosphere is such that,
As I look abroad upon the length and breadth of the land,
It recedes from my eye,
And I seem to be looking for the threads of velvet.

Now first mark the stubble
And numerous withered weeds rising above the snow.
They have suddenly aquired a new character.

Tansy still shows its yellow disks,
But yarrow is particularly fresh and perfect,
Cold and chaste,
With its pretty little dry-looking rounded white petals
And green leaves.
Its very color gives it a right to bloom above the snow, —
As level as a snow-crust on the top of the stubble.
It looks like a virgin wearing a white ruff.

NOVEMBER

The jay is the bird of October.

I have seen it repeatedly flitting amid the bright leaves,
Of a different color from them all and equally bright,
And taking its flight from grove to grove.
It, too, with its bright color,
Stands for some ripeness in the bird harvest.

And its scream!
It is as if it blowed on the edge of an October leaf.

I saw a muskrat come out of a hole in the ice.
He is a man wilder than Ray or Melvin.
While I am looking at him,
I am thinking what he is thinking of me.
He is a different sort of man, that is all.

He would dive when I went nearer,
Then reappear again,
And had kept open a place five or six feet square
So that it had not frozen, by swimming about in it.

Then he would sit on the edge of the ice
And busy himself about something,
I could not see whether it was a clam or not.

What a cold-blooded fellow!
Thoughts at a low temperature,
Sitting perfectly still so long on ice covered with water,
Mumbling a cold, wet clam in its shell.

This is my music each evening.
I heard it last evening.
The men who help me call it the "hooting owl"
And think it is the cat owl.
It is a sound admirably suited [to] the swamp
And to the twilight woods,
Suggesting a vast undeveloped nature
Which men have not recognized nor satisfied.

I rejoice that there are owls.
They represent the stark, twilight,
Unsatisfied thoughts I have.
Let owls do the idiotic and maniacal hooting for men.

A still, cold night.
The light of the rising moon in the east.
Moonrise is a faint sunrise.
And what shall we name the faint aurora
That precedes the moonrise?

The ground is frozen and echoes to my tread.
There are absolutely no crickets to be heard now.
They are heard, then, till the ground freezes.

To-day I heard for the first time this season
The crackling, vibrating sound which resounds from thin ice
When a stone is cast upon it.
So far have we got toward winter.
It is doubtful if they who have not pulled their turnips
Will have a chance to get them.
It is not of much use to drive the cows to pasture.
I can fancy that I hear the booming of ice in the ponds.

No Indian summer have we had this November.
I see but few traces of the perennial spring.
Now is there nothing, not even the cold beauty
Of ice crystals and snowy architecture,
Nothing but the echo of your steps over the frozen ground,
No voice of birds nor frogs.

You are dry as a farrow cow.
The earth will not admit a spade.
All fields lie fallow.

WINTER

DECEMBER

DECEMBER

If it were not for the light reflected from the snow
It would be quite dark.
The woodchopper has started for home.
I can no longer distinguish the color of the red oak leaves
Against the snow,
But they appear black.
The partridges have come forth to bud on the apple trees.

Now the sun has quite disappeared,
But the afterglow, as I may call it,
Apparently the reflection from the cloud
Beyond which the sun went down
On the thick atmosphere of the horizon,
Is unusually bright and lasting.

Long, broken clouds in the horizon,
In the dun atmosphere, –
As if the fires of day were still smoking there, –
Hang with a red and golden edging
Like the saddlecloths of the steeds of the sun.

The large leafy lichens on the white pines,
Especially on the outside of the wood,
Look almost a golden yellow
In the light reflected from the snow,
While deeper in the woods they are ash-colored.

In the swamps
The dry, yellowish-colored fruit of the poison dogwood
Hangs like jewelry on long, drooping stems.
It is pleasant to meet it,
It has so much character relatively to man.

Here is a stump on which a squirrel has sat
And stripped the pine cones of a neighboring tree.
Their cores and scales lie all around.
He knew that they contained an almond
Before the naturalist did.
He has long been a close observer of Nature;
Opens her caskets.

The notes of the wood thrush
And the sound of a vibrating chord,
These affect me as many sounds once did often,
And as almost all should.

The strains of the aeolian harp and of the wood thrush
Are the truest and loftiest preachers that I know
Now left on this earth.
I know of no missionaries to us heathen comparable to them.
They, as it were, lift us up in spite of ourselves.
They intoxicate, they charm us.

Where was that strain mixed
Into which this world was dropped but as a lump of sugar
To sweeten the draught?

DECEMBER

How much, what infinite, leisure it requires,
As of a lifetime,
To appreciate a single phenomenon!

You must camp down beside it as for life,
Having reached your land of promise,
And give yourself wholly to it.

It must stand for the whole world to you,
Symbolical of all things.
The least partialness is your own defect of sight
And cheapens the experience fatally.

Unless the humming of a gnat
Is as the music of the spheres,
And the music of the spheres
Is as the humming of a gnat,
They are naught to me.

Few eyes have rested on him hooting;
Few on him silent on his perch even.

Yet cut away the woods never so much year after year,
Though the chopper has not seen him
And only a grove or two is left,
Still his aboriginal voice is heard
Indefinitely far and sweet,
Mingled oft, in strange harmony,
With the newly invented din of trade,
Like a sentence of Allegri sounded in our streets, –
Hooting from invisible perch at his foes
The woodchoppers,
Who are invading his domains.

Foxes are forest dogs.
I hear one barking raggedly,
Wildly,
Demoniacally in the darkness to-night,
Seeking expression,
Laboring with some anxiety,
Striving to be a dog outright
That he may carelessly run in the street,
Struggling for light.

He is but a faint man,
Before pygmies;
An imperfect, burrowing man.
He has come up near to my window,
Attracted by the light,
And barked a vulpine curse at me,
Then retreated.

I observed this afternoon the old Irishwoman
At the shanty in the woods,
Sitting out on the hillside,
Bare-headed, in the rain
And on the icy though thawing ground,
Knitting.
She comes out, like the ground squirrel,
At the least intimation of warmer weather.
She will not have to go far to be buried,
So close she lives to the earth.

DECEMBER

I see a great many barrels and fig-drums
And piles of wood for umbrella-sticks
And blocks of granite and ice, etc.,
And that is Boston.

Great piles of goods
And the means of packing and conveying them,
Much wrapping-paper and twine,
Many crates and hogsheads and trucks,
That is Boston.

The more barrels, the more Boston.

Let us walk in the world without learning its ways.
Whole weeks or months of my summer life slide away
In thin volumes like mist or smoke,
Till at length some warm morning, perchance,
I see a sheet of mist blown down the brook to the swamp,
Its shadow flitting across the fields,
Which have caught a new significance from that accident;
And as that vapor is raised above the earth,
So shall the next weeks be elevated
Above the plane of the actual;
Or when the setting sun slants across the pastures,
And the cows low to my inward ear
And only enhance the stillness,
And the eve is as the dawn,
A beginning hour and not a final one,
As if it would never have done,
With its clear western amber
Inciting men to lives of as limpid purity.

Then do other parts of my day's work shine
Than I had thought at noon,
For I discover the real purport of my toil,
As, when the husbandman has reached the end of the furrow
And looks back,
He can best tell where the pressed earth shines most.

JANUARY

This is one of those pleasant winter mornings
When you find the river firmly frozen in the night,
But still the air is serene
And the sun feels gratefully warm
An hour after sunrise, – though so fair,
A healthy whitish vapor fills the lower stratum of the air,
Concealing the mountains, –
The smokes go up from the village,
You hear the cocks with immortal vigor,
And the children shout on their way to school,
And the sound made by the railroad men
Hammering a rail is uncommonly musical.

You lie with your feet or legs curled up,
Waiting for morning,
The sheets shining with frost about your mouth.

Water left by the stove is frozen thickly,
And what you sprinkle in bathing falls on the floor ice.
The house plants are all frozen
And soon droop and turn black.

I look out on the roof of a cottage
Covered a foot deep with snow,
Wondering how the poor children in its garret,
With their few rags,
Contrive to keep their toes warm.

I mark the white smoke from its chimney,
Whose contracted wreaths are soon dissipated
In this stinging air,
And think of the size of their wood-pile,
And again I try to realize how they panted
For a breath of cool air those sultry nights last summer.

Realize it now if you can.
Recall the hum of the mosquito.

Every leaf and twig was this morning
Covered with a sparkling ice armor;
Even the grasses in exposed fields were hung
With innumerable diamond pendants,
Which jingled merrily when brushed
By the foot of the traveller.

It was literally the wreck of jewels
And the crash of gems.
It was as though some superincumbent stratum of the earth
Had been removed in the night,
Exposing to light a bed of untarnished crystals.

The scene changed at every step,
Or as the head was inclined to the right or the left.
There were the opal and sapphire
And emerald and jasper
And beryl and topaz
And ruby.

Such is beauty ever, — neither here nor there,
Now nor then, —
Neither in Rome nor in Athens,
But wherever there is a soul to admire.

Is its trail too old?
Have mortals lost the scent?
The great game for mighty hunters
As soon as the first snow falls is Purity,
For, earlier than any rabbit or fox, it is abroad,
And its trail may be detected by curs of lowest degree.

Did this great snow come
To reveal the track merely of some timorous hare,
Or of the Great Hare,
Whose track no hunter has seen?

How snug they are somewhere under the snow now,
Not to be thought of, if it were not for these pretty tracks!
And for a week, or fortnight even,
Of pretty still weather the tracks will remain,
To tell of the nocturnal adventures of a tiny mouse
Who was not beneath the notice of the Lord.

So it was so many thousands of years
Before Gutenberg invented printing with *his* types,
And so it will be so many thousands of years
After his types are forgotten, perchance.
The deer mouse will be printing
On the snow of Well Meadow
To be read by a new race of men.

No music from the telegraph harp on the causeway,
Where the wind is strong,
But in the Cut this cold day I hear memorable strains.

What must the birds and beasts think
Where it passes through woods,
Who heard only the squeaking of the trees before!
I should think that these strains
Would get into their music at last.
Will not the mockingbird be heard one day
Inserting this strain in his medley?

It intoxicates me.
Orpheus is still alive.
All poetry and mythology revive.
The spirits of all bards sweep the strings.
I hear the clearest silver, lyre-like tones.

When approaching the pond yesterday,
Through my bean-field,
I saw where some fishermen had come away,
And the tails of their string of pickerel
Had trailed on the deep snow where they sank in it.

I afterward saw where they had been fishing that forenoon,
The water just beginning to freeze,
And also where some had fished the day before
With red-finned minnows,
Which were frozen into an inch of ice;
That these men had chewed tobacco and ate apples.

All this I knew,
Though I saw neither man nor squirrel
Nor pickerel nor crow.

Now I go a-fishing and a-hunting every day,
But omit the fish and the game,
Which are the least important part.
I have learned to do without them.
They were indispensable only as long as I was a boy.

I am encouraged
When I see a dozen villagers drawn to Walden Pond
To spend a day in fishing through the ice,
And suspect that I have more fellows than I knew,
But I am disappointed and surprised
To find that they lay all stress on the fish
Which they catch or fail to catch,
And on nothing else,
As if there were nothing else to be caught.

I have had but two or three invitations to lecture in a year,
And some years none at all.
I congratulate myself
On having been permitted to stay at home thus,
I am so much richer for it.

I do not see what I should have got of much value,
But money, by going about,
But I do see what I should have lost.
It seems to me
That I have a longer
And more liberal lease of life thus.

I cannot afford to be telling my experience,
Especially to those who perhaps will take no interest in it.
I wish to be getting experience.

You might as well recommend to a bear
To leave his hollow tree and run about all winter
Scratching at all the hollow trees in the woods.
He would be leaner in the spring
Than if he had stayed at home and sucked his claws.

JANUARY

It is a fair sunset,
With many purplish fishes in the horizon,
Pinkish and golden with bright edges;
Like a school of purplish whales,
They sail or float down from the north;
Or like leopards' skins
They hang in the west.

We never tire of the drama of sunset.
I go forth each afternoon and look into the west
A quarter of an hour before sunset, with fresh curiosity,
To see what new picture will be painted there,
What new panorama exhibited,
What new dissolving views.
Can Washington Street or Broadway show anything as good?
Every day a new picture is painted and framed,
Held up for half an hour,
In such lights as the Great Artist chooses,
And then withdrawn,
And the curtain falls.

And then the sun goes down,
And long the afterglow gives light.
And then the damask curtains glow
Along the western window.
And now the first star is lit,
And I go home.

FEBRUARY

Then there is the wonderful stillness of a winter day.
The sources of sound as of water, are frozen up;
Scarcely a tinkling rill of it is to be heard.
When we listen,
We hear only that sound of the surf of our internal sea,
Rising and swelling in our ears as in two seashells.
It is the sabbath of the year, stillness audible.

All day a steady, warm, imprisoning rain
Carrying off the snow,
Not unmusical on my roof.

It is a rare time for the student and reader
Who cannot go abroad in the afternoon,
Provided he can keep awake,
For we are wont to be drowsy as cats in such weather.

Without, it is not walking but wading.
It is so long since I have heard it that the steady,
Soaking,
Rushing sound of the rain on the shingles is musical.
The fire needs no replenishing, and we save our fuel.
It seems like a distant forerunner of spring.

It is because I am allied to the elements
That the sound of the rain is thus soothing to me.
The sound soaks into my spirit,
As the water into the earth,
Reminding me of the season
When snow and ice will be no more,
When the earth will be thawed
And drink up the rain as fast as it falls.

I trust that the walkers of the present day
Are conscious of the blessings which they enjoy
In the comparative freedom
With which they can ramble over the country
And enjoy the landscape,
Anticipating with compassion that future day
When possibly it will be partitioned off
Into so-called pleasure-grounds,
Where only a few may enjoy
The narrow and exclusive pleasure
Which is compatible with ownership, –
When walking over the surface of God's earth
Shall be construed to mean trespassing
On some gentleman's grounds,
When fences shall be multiplied
And man traps and other engines invented
To confine men to the public road.

I have lived some thirty-odd years on this planet,
And I have yet to hear the first syllable of valuable
Or even earnest advice from my seniors.
They have told me nothing,
And probably can tell me nothing to the purpose.

There is life,
An experiment untried by me,
And it does not avail me that you have tried it.
If I have any valuable experience,
I am sure to reflect that this my mentors said nothing about.
What were mysteries to the child
Remain mysteries to the old man.

I feel, of course, very ignorant in a museum.
I know nothing about the things which they have there, —
No more than I should know my friends in the tomb.

I walk amid those jars of bloated creatures
Which they label frogs,
A total stranger,
Without the least froggy thought being suggested.
Not one of them can croak.
They leave behind all life they that enter there,
Both frogs and men.

The bluebird does not come
Till the air consents
And his wedge will enter easily.
The air over these fields
Is a foundry full of moulds
For casting bluebirds' warbles.

Any sound uttered now would take that form,
Not of the harsh, vibrating, rending scream of the jay,
But a softer, flowing, curling warble,
Like a purling stream
Or the lobes of flowing sand and clay.

Here is the soft air and the moist expectant apple trees,
But not yet the bluebird.

When I perceive this dryness under my feet,
I feel as if I had got a new sense,
Or rather I realize what was incredible to me before,
That there is a new life in Nature beginning to awake,
That her halls are being swept
And prepared for a new occupant.

It is whispered through all the aisles of the forest
That another spring is approaching.
The wood mouse listens at the mouth of his burrow,
And the chickadee passes the news along.

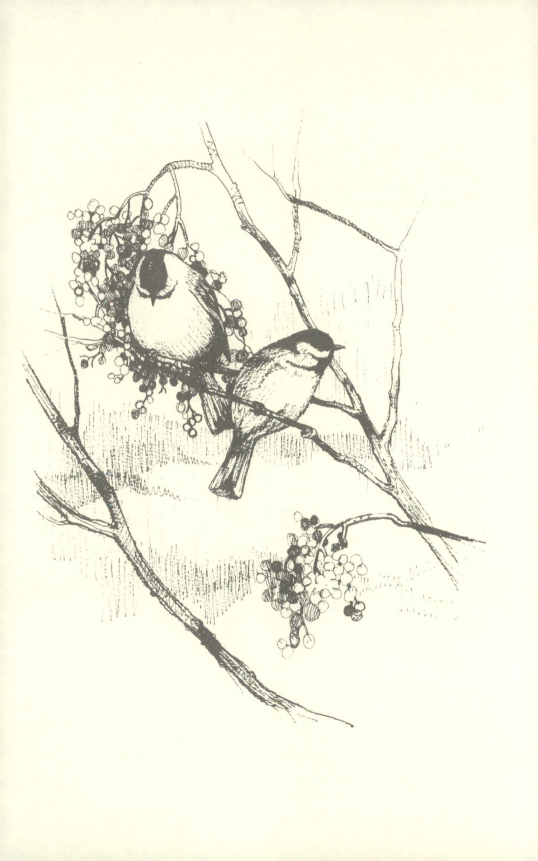

The hen-hawk and the pine are friends.
The same thing which keeps the hen-hawk in the woods,
Away from the cities,
Keeps me here.

That bird settles with confidence on a white pine top
And not upon your weathercock.
That bird will not be poultry of yours,
Lays no eggs for you,
Forever hides its nest.

SPRING

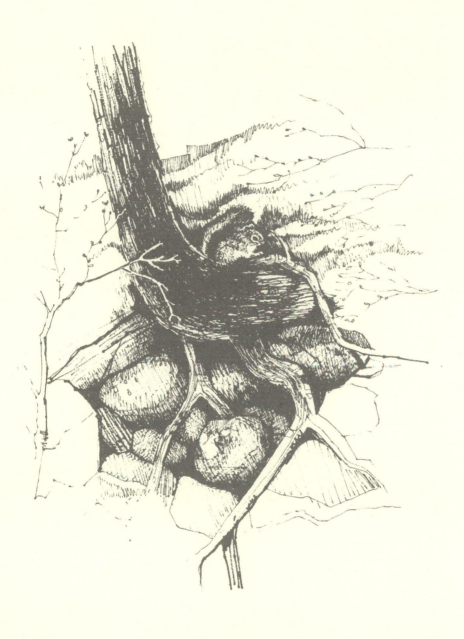

MARCH

The boy's sled gets put away in the barn or shed or garret,
And there lies dormant all summer,
Like a woodchuck in the winter.
It goes into its burrow just before woodchucks come out,
So that you may say a woodchuck never sees a sled,
Nor a sled a woodchuck, –
Unless it were a prematurely risen woodchuck
Or a belated and unseasonable sled.
Before the woodchuck comes out the sled goes in.
They dwell at the antipodes of each other.
Before sleds rise woodchucks have set.

When only the snow had begun to melt
And no rill of song had broken loose,
A note so dry and fettered still,
So inarticulate and half thawed out,
That you might (and would commonly)
Mistake for the tapping of a woodpecker.
As if the young nuthatch in its hole
Had listened only to the tapping of woodpeckers
And learned that music, and now,
When it would sing and give vent to its spring ecstasy,
It can modulate only some notes like that.
That is its theme still.
That is its ruling idea of song and music, —
Only a little clangor and liquidity
Added to the tapping of the woodpecker.

MARCH

It is a good plan to go to some old orchard
On the south side of a hill,
Sit down, and listen,
Especially in the morning when all is still.

You can thus often hear the distant warble
Of some bluebird lately arrived,
Which, if you had been walking,
Would not have been audible to you.

As I walk, these first mild spring days.
With my coat thrown open,
Stepping over tinkling rills of melting snow,
Excited by the sight of bare ground,
Especially the reddish subsoil,
Where it is exposed by a cutting,
And by the few green radical leaves,
I stand still, shut my eyes,
And listen from time to time,
In order to hear the note of some bird of passage
Just arrived.

His Most Serene Birdship!
His soft warble melts in the ear,
As the snow is melting in the valleys around.
The bluebird comes
And with his warble drills the ice
And sets free the rivers and ponds and frozen ground.
As the sand flows down the slopes a little way,
Assuming the forms of foliage
Where the frost comes out of the ground,
So this little rill of melody
Flows a short way down the concave of the sky.

MARCH

I no sooner step out of the house
Than I hear the bluebirds in the air,
And far and near, everywhere except in the woods,
Throughout the town you may hear them, —
The blue curls of their warblings, —
Harbingers of serene and warm weather,
Little azure rills of melody
Trickling here and there from out the air,
Their short warble trilled in the air
Reminding of so many corkscrews
Assaulting and thawing the torpid mass of winter,
Assisting the ice and snow to melt
And the streams to flow.

Now I see and hear the lark
Sitting with head erect, neck outstretched,
In the middle of a pasture,
And I hear another far off singing.

Sing when they first come.
All these birds do their warbling
Especially in the still, sunny hour after sunrise,
As rivers twinkle at their sources.

Now is the time to be abroad and hear them,
As you detect the slightest ripple in smooth water.
As with tinkling sounds
The sources of streams burst their icy fetters,
So the rills of music begin to flow
And swell the general quire of spring.

I then see a bird alight
On the dead top of the highest white oak on the hilltop,
On the topmost point.
It is a shrike.

While I am watching him eight or ten rods off,
I hear robins down below, west of the hill.
Then, to my surprise, the shrike begins to sing.

It is at first a wholly ineffectual and inarticulate sound
Without any solid tone to it,
A mere hoarse breathing, as if he were clearing his throat,
Unlike any bird that I know, —a shrill hissing.

Then he uttered a kind of mew,
A very decided mewing, clear and wiry,
Between that of a catbird and the note of a nuthatch,
As if to lure a nuthatch within his reach;
Then rose into the sharpest, shrillest
Vibratory or tremulous whistling
Or chirruping on the very highest key.
This high gurging jingle was like some of the notes
Of a robin singing in summer.

The song sparrow
And the transient fox-colored sparrow, —
Have they brought me no message this year?
Do they go to lead heroic lives in Rupert's Land?

They are so small,
I think their destinies must be large.
Have I heard what this tiny passenger has to say,
While it flits thus from tree to tree?

Suddenly I look up and see a new bird,
Probably an eagle, quite above me,
Laboring with the wind not more than forty rods off.
It was the largest bird of the falcon kind I ever saw.
I was never so impressed by any flight.

She sailed the air,
And fell back from time to time
Like a ship on her beam ends,
Holding her talons up
As if ready for the arrows.

Some, seeing and admiring the neat figure of the hawk
Sailing two or three hundred feet above their heads,
Wish to get nearer and hold it in their hands, perchance,
Not realizing that they can see it best at this distance,
Better now, perhaps, than ever they will again.
What is an eagle in captivity! —
Screaming in a courtyard!
I am not the wiser respecting eagles
For having seen one there.
I do not wish to know the length of its entrails.

MARCH

Heard two hawks scream.
There was something truly March-like in it,
Like a prolonged blast or whistling of the wind
Through a crevice in the sky,
Which, like a cracked blue saucer, overlaps the woods.
Such are the first rude notes
Which prelude the summer's quire,
Learned of the whistling March wind.

Found on the Great Fields
A fragment of Indian soapstone ware,
Which, judging from its curve and thinness,
For a vestige of the rim remains,
Was a dish of the form and size of a saucer,
Only three times as thick.

Listening for early birds,
I hear a faint tinkling sound in the leafless woods,
As if a piece of glass rattled against a stone.

MARCH

Saw a skunk in the Corner road,
Which I followed sixty rods or more.
Out now about 4 P.M., —
Partly because it is a dark, foul day.

It is a slender black (and white) animal,
With its back remarkably arched,
Standing high behind and carrying its head low;
Runs, even when undisturbed,
With a singular teeter or undulation,
Like the walking of a Chinese lady.

My Aunt Maria asked me to read the life of Dr. Chalmers,
Which however I did not promise to do.
Yesterday, Sunday, she was heard through the partition
Shouting to my Aunt Jane, who is deaf,
"Think of it!
He stood half an hour to-day to hear the frogs croak,
And he wouldn't read the life of Chalmers."

APRIL

Here, where I come for the earliest flowers,
I might also come for the earliest birds.
They seek the same warmth and vegetation.
And so probably with quadrupeds, –
Rabbits, skunks, mice, etc.

I hear now, as I stand over the first skunk-cabbage,
The notes of the first red-wings,
Like the squeaking of a sign,
Over amid the maples yonder.

Robins are peeping and flitting about.
Am surprised to hear one sing regularly
Their morning strain,
Seven or eight rods off,
Yet so low and smothered with its ventriloquism
That you would say it was half a mile off.
It seems to be wooing its mate,
That sits within a foot of it.

The wood thrush afar, –
So superior a strain to that of other birds.
I was doubting if it would affect me as of yore,
But it did measurably.
I did not believe there could be such differences.

This is the gospel according to the wood thrush.
He makes a sabbath out of a week-day.
I could go to hear him,
Could buy a pew in his church.

The first partridge drums in one or two places,
As if the earth's pulse now beat audibly
With the increased flow of life.
It slightly flutters all Nature
And makes her heart palpitate.

Also, as I stand listening for the wren,
And sweltering in my greatcoat,
I hear the woods filled with the hum of insects,
As if my hearing were affected;
And thus the summer's quire begins.

The silent spaces have begun to be filled
With notes of birds and insects
And the peep and croak and snore of frogs,
Even as living green blades are everywhere
Pushing up amid the sere ones.

The note of the pine warbler.
It sounds far off and faint,
But, coming out and sitting on the iron rail,
I am surprised to see it within three or four rods,
On the upper part of a white oak,
Where it is busily catching insects,
Hopping along toward the extremities of the limbs
And looking off on all sides,
Twice darting off like a wood pewee,
Two rods, over the railroad,
After an insect and returning to the oak,
And from time to time uttering its simple,
Rapidly iterated,
Cool-sounding notes.

When heard a little within the wood,
As he hops to that side of the oak,
They sound particularly cool and inspiring,
Like a part of the evergreen forest itself,
The trickling of the sap.

The bay-wing now sings —
The first I have been able to hear —
Both about the Texas house
And the fields this side of Hayden's,
Both of them similar dry and open pastures.

I heard it just before noon,
When the sun began to come out, and at 3 P.M.,
Singing loud and clear and incessantly.
It sings with a pleasing deliberation,
Contrasting with the spring vivacity of the song sparrow,
Whose song many would confound it with.

It comes to revive with its song
The dry uplands and pastures
And grass-fields about the skirts of villages.
Only think how finely our life is furnished
In all its details, —
Sweet wild birds
Provided to fill its interstices with song!

This warbler impresses me
As if it were calling the trees to life.
I think of springing twigs.

Its jingle rings through the woods at short intervals,
As if, like an electric shock,
It imparted a fresh spring life to them.

You hear the same bird, now here now there,
As it incessantly flits about,
Commonly invisible and uttering its simple jingle
On very different keys,
And from time to time a companion is heard
Farther or nearer.

This is a peculiarly summer-like sound.
Go to a warm pine wood-side on a pleasant day
At this season after storm,
And hear it ring with the jingle of the pine warbler.

The rain was soothing,
So still and sober,
Gently beating against and amusing our thoughts,
Swelling the brooks.

The robin now peeps with scared note
In the heavy overcast air,
Among the apple trees.
The hour is favorable to thought.

Such a day I like a sandy road,
Snows that melt and leave bare the corn and grain fields,
With Indian relics shining on them,
And prepare the ground for the farmer.

As I go down the street just after sunset,
I hear many snipe to-night.

This sound is annually heard by the villagers,
But always at this hour, *i.e.* in the twilight, —
A hovering sound high in the air, —
And they do not know what to refer it to.
It is very easily imitated by the breath.
A sort of shuddering with the breath.

It reminds me of calmer nights.
Hardly one in a hundred hears it,
And perhaps not nearly so many know
What creature makes it.

Perhaps no one dreamed of snipe an hour ago,
But the air seemed empty of such as they;
But as soon as the dusk begins,
So that a bird's flight is concealed,
You hear this peculiar spirit-suggesting sound,
Now far, now near,
Heard through and above the evening din of the village.

At Hemlock Brook,
A dozen or more rods from the river,
I see on the wet mud a little snapping turtle
Evidently hatched last year.

It does not open its eyes nor mouth while I hold it.
Its eyes appear as if sealed up by its long sleep.

In our ability to contend with the elements
What feeble infants we are to this one.
Talk of great heads, look at this one!
Talk of Hercules' feats in the cradle,
What sort of Cradle and nursing has this infant had?
It totters forth confident and victorious
When it can hardly carry its shield.

The water on the meadows is now quite high
On account of the melting snow and the rain.
It makes a lively prospect when the wind blows,
Where our summer meads spread, –
A tumultuous sea,
A myriad waves breaking with whitecaps
Like gambolling sheep,
For want of other comparison in the country.

Far and wide a sea of motion,
Schools of porpoises,
Lines of Virgil realized.
One would think it a novel sight for inland meadows.

Where the cranberry and andromeda
And swamp white oak and maple grow,
Here is a mimic sea, with its gulls.
At the bottom of the sea, cranberries.

The goose sailing on our waters,
Or the great heron feeding here.
When the storm increases, then these great birds
That carry the mail of the seasons lay to.
To see wild life you must go forth at a wild season.

When it rains and blows, keeping men indoors,
Then the lover of Nature must forth.
Then returns Nature to her wild estate.

In pleasant sunny weather you may catch butterflies,
But only when the storm rages
That lays prostrate the forest and wrecks the mariner,
Do you come upon the feeding-grounds of wildest fowl, —
Of heron and geese.

Our Concord River is a dead stream
In more senses than we had supposed.
In what sense now does the spring ever come to the river,
When the sun is not reflected from the scales
Of a single salmon, shad, or alewife?

No doubt there is *some* compensation for this loss,
But I do not at this moment see clearly what it is.
That river which the aboriginal and indigenous fishes
Have not deserted
Is a more primitive and interesting river to me.
It is as if some vital quality were to be lost
Out of a man's blood
And it were to circulate
More lifelessly through his veins.

What a pitiful business is the fur trade,
Which has been pursued now for so many ages,
For so many years by famous companies
Which enjoy a profitable monopoly
And control a large portion of the earth's surface,
Unweariedly pursuing and ferreting out small animals
By the aid of the loafing class
Tempted by rum and money,
That you may rob some little fellow-creature of its coat
To adorn or thicken your own,
That you may get a fashionable covering
In which to hide your head,
Or a suitable robe
In which to dispense justice to your fellow-men!

You will meet the most tender-hearted
And delicately bred lady,
Perhaps the President of the Antislavery Society,
Or of that for the encouragement of humanity to animals,
Marching or presiding
With the scales from a tortoise's back —
Obtained by laying live coals on it to make them curl up —
Stuck in her hair,
Rat–skin fitting as close to her fingers as erst to the rat,
And, for her cloak, trimmings
Perchance adorned with the spoils of a hundred skunks, —
Rendered inodorous, we trust.
Poor misguided woman!
Could she not wear other armor in the war of humanity?

Indians follow the buffaloes;
Trout, suckers, etc., follow the water-bugs, etc.;
Reptiles follow vegetation, insects, and worms;
Birds of prey, the flycatchers etc.
Man follows all,
And all follow the sun.

MAY

MAY

I have passed the Rubicon of staying out.
I have said to myself, that way is not homeward;
I will wander further from what I have called my home —
To the home which is forever inviting me.

In such an hour the freedom of the woods is offered me,
And the birds sing my dispensation.

First observe the creak of crickets.
It is quite general amid these rocks.
The song of only one is more interesting to me.

It suggests lateness,
But only as we come to a knowledge of eternity
After some acquaintance with time.
It is only late for all trivial and hurried pursuits.

It suggests a wisdom mature, never late,
Being above all temporal considerations,
Which possesses the coolness and maturity of autumn
Amidst the aspiration of spring
And the heats of summer.

To the birds they say:
"Ah! you speak like children from impulse;
Nature speaks through you;
But with us it is ripe knowledge.
The seasons do not revolve for us;
We sing their lullaby."
So they chant,
Eternal, at the roots of the grass.

MAY

The red-eye at the spring;
Quite a woodland note.
The different moods or degrees of wildness and poetry
Of which the song of birds is the keynote.

The wood thrush Mr. Barnum never hired nor can,
Though he could bribe Jenny Lind
And put her into his cage.

How many little birds of the warbler family are busy now
About the opening buds,
While I sit by the spring!
They are almost as much a part of the tree
As its blossoms and leaves.
They come and give it voice.

The wood thrush has sung for some time.
He touches a depth in me
Which no other bird's song does.
He has learned to sing,
And no thrumming of the strings or tuning disturbs you.

Other birds may whistle pretty well,
But he is the master of a finer-toned instrument.
His song is musical,
Not from association merely,
Not from variety,
But the character of its tone.

It is all divine, –
A Shakespeare among birds,
And a Homer too.

At Loring's Wood heard and saw a tanager.
That contrast of a *red* bird
With the green pines and the blue sky!

Even when I have heard his note
And look for him
And find the bloody fellow,
Sitting on a dead twig of a pine,
I am always startled.
(They seem to love the darkest and thickest pines.)

That incredible red,
With the green and blue,
As if these were the trinity we wanted.

Yet with his hoarse note he pays for his color.
I am transported;
These are not the woods I ordinarily walk in.
He sunk Concord in his thought.
How he enhances the wildness and wealth of the woods!

By owl-nest tree.
The parti-colored warbler is very common
And musical there, — my tweezer bird, —
Making the *screep screep screep* note.

It is an almost incessant singer
And a very handsomely marked bird.
It frequents the spruce trees,
At regular intervals pausing as it flits, hops,
And creeps about from limb to limb or up the main stem,
And holding up its head,
Utters its humble notes.

MAY

In Boston yesterday
An ornithologist said significantly,
"If you held the bird in your hand—"
But I would rather hold it in my affections.

I hear from some far meadow bay,
Across the Great meadows,
The half-sounded trump of a bullfrog this warm morning.

It is like the top of a drum
When human legions are mustering.
It reminds me that summer is now in earnest
Mustering her forces,
And that ere long I shall see their waving plumes
And glancing armor
And hear the full bands and steady tread.

The bullfrog is earth's trumpeter,
At the head of the terrene band.
He replies to the sky with answering thunder.

MAY

Going through the Depot Field,
I hear the dream frog at a distance.

The little peeping frogs make a background
Of sound in the horizon,
Which you do not hear
Unless you attend.

The former is a trembling note, some higher,
Some lower, along the edge of the earth,
An all-pervading sound.

Nearer, it is a blubbering or rather bubbling sound,
Such as children,
Who stand nearer to nature,
Can and do often make, —
This and many others,
Remembering the frog state.

Thimble-berry two or three days.
Cattle stand in the river by the bridge for coolness.
Place my hat lightly on my head
That the air may circulate beneath.

Wild roses budded before you know it—
Will be out often before you know they are budded.

Fields are whitened with mouse-ear gone to seed—
A mass of white fuzz blowing off one side—
And also with dandelion globes of seeds.
Some plants have already reached their fall.

How still the hot noon;
People have retired behind blinds.

Yet the kingbird—lively bird,
With white belly and tail edged with white,
And with its lively twittering—
Stirs and keeps the air brisk.

MAY

It is glorious to stand in the midst of the andromeda,
Which so level and thick fills the swamp,
And look up at the blue spruce trees.

The edges of the scales of the young cones,
Which are at the tops of the trees
(Where the branches make light and open crosses),
Seen against the sunlit sky
Or against the light merely, being transparent,
Are a splendid crimson color,
As if the condensed fire of all sunsets
Were reflected from them, like the richest damask
Or ruby-throated hummingbird's breast.

We soon get through with Nature.
She excites an expectation which she cannot satisfy.

The merest child which has rambled into a copsewood
Dreams of a wilderness so wild
And strange and inexhaustible
As Nature can never show him.

The red-bird
Which I saw on my companion's string on election days
I thought but the outmost sentinel
Of the wild, immortal camp, —
Of the wild and dazzling infantry of the wilderness, —
That the deeper woods abounded with redder birds still;
But, now that I have threaded all our woods
And waded the swamps,
I have never yet met with his compeer,
Still less his wilder kindred.

The red-bird
Which is the last of Nature
Is but the first of God.

MAY

Now is the summer come.
A breezy, washing day.
A day for shadows, even of moving clouds,
Over fields in which the grass is beginning to wave.

Senecio in bloom.
A bird's nest in grass,
With coffee-colored eggs.
Cinquefoil and houstonia cover the ground,
Mixed with the grass
And contrasting with each other.
Strong lights and shades now.

Wild cherry on the low shrubs,
But not yet the trees,
A rummy scent.

First Line of Poem
Date of JOURNAL Entry

WILLIAM M. WHITE is Professor of English and Coordinator of the Creative Writing Program at Virginia Polytechnic Institute and State University. His scholarly and critical articles on American Literature have appeared in such journals as *Forum, Sewanee Review* and the *Thoreau Journal Quarterly*. His short stories and poems have been widely published during the past fifteen years. He is presently working on a novel and AT ONE WITH THE UNIVERSE, the final collection of found poems from Thoreau's *Journals*.

STEVE ADAMS is Assistant Professor of English at Virginia Polytechnic Institute and State University and is widely recognized for his contributions to Thoreau scholarship.

GEORGIA W. DEARBORN lives and works on Cape Cod, in Harwichport, MA, where she and her husband own an art gallery featuring her works and the works of other Cape artists. A talented artist, she is well known for her pen and ink illustrations for several major publishers and for her watercolor and acrylic paintings of wild life, florals, the English Countryside, and Cape Cod scenes.

2012